IMMIGRATION POLICY

Other Books in the At Issue Series:

- Environmental Justice
- Ethnic Conflict
- Policing the Police
- Rape on Campus
- Smoking
- What Is Sexual Harassment?